STECK-VAUGHN

LIFE Skills

FOR TODAY'S WORLD

BY VIVIAN BERNSTEIN

Money and Consumers

CONSULTANTS

Dee Marie Boydstun
Literacy Coordinator
Black Hawk College
Moline, Illinois

Marie S. Olsen
Learning Center Coordinator
for Rio Salado Community College
at Maricopa Skill Center
Phoenix, Arizona

John C. Ritter
Teacher, Education Programs
Oregon Women's Correctional Center
Salem, Oregon

STECK-VAUGHN
COMPANY
A Subsidiary of National Education Corporation

ABOUT THE AUTHOR

Vivian Bernstein is the author of *America's Story, World History and You, World Geography and You, American Government,* and *Decisions for Health.* She received her Master of Arts degree from New York University. Bernstein is active with professional organizations in social studies, education, and reading. She gives presentations to school faculties and professional groups about content area reading. Bernstein was a teacher in the New York City Public School System for a number of years.

ACKNOWLEDGMENTS

Executive Editor: Diane Sharpe
Project Editor: Anne Souby
Designer: Pamela Heaney
Photo Editor: Margie Foster
Production: American Composition & Graphics, Inc.

CREDITS

All photos by Park Street with the following exceptions.
Cover (forms) Cooke Photographics; p. 6 Reagan Bradshaw; p. 16 © David Young Wolfe/PhotoEdit; pp. 17, 18 Reagan Bradshaw; p. 27 © Peter Gridley/FPG; p. 28 © Tony Freeman/PhotoEdit; pp. 47, 48, 49, 66 Reagan Bradshaw; p. 67 © Bob Dammrich/Stock Boston; p. 68 © John Coletti/Stock Boston; p. 69 © Spencer Grant/Stock Boston.

Credit card application form and car loan application form reproduced with the permission of Citibank.

PRINTED WITH
SOY INK

CONTENTS

Life Skills for Today's World is a series of five books. These books are *Money and Consumers*, *The World of Work*, *Your Own Home*, *Personal Health*, and *Community and Government*. They can help you learn skills to be successful in today's world and will show you how to use these skills in your daily life.

This book is *Money and Consumers*. A **consumer** is a person who buys and uses products and services. You are a consumer every time you buy something at a store. You are a consumer every time you make a phone call.

Each chapter in this book has six pages of lesson text. This text is followed by a workshop and exercises. One workshop in this book is "Completing a Credit Card Application." What kind of applications have you filled out?

_____

_____

_____

In the "Thinking and Writing" exercise, you will be asked to write in your journal. Your journal can be a notebook or just a group of papers. Writing in a journal helps you gather your thoughts and put them on paper. One exercise in this book asks you to think about how you shop. It asks you to think about how you decide what to buy and how you can become a better shopper. Thinking and writing about problems can help you find answers. Try it here. Think about questions or problems you may have about money. On the lines below, tell how you think this book will help you.

_____

_____

_____

_____

There are an index, a glossary, and an answer key in the back of this book. These features can help you use this book independently. Have fun working through this book. Then enjoy your new skills!

USING BANKING SERVICES

Think About As You Read

▶ Why would you want to have a savings account or a checking account?

▶ How do you open a savings account or a checking account?

▶ How do you choose a bank?

Michael is now earning enough money to save part of every paycheck. He thought about opening a **savings account** at a bank. He knew his savings would earn **interest** in the bank. Because of this interest, the money that Michael put into his savings account would earn more money for him. Michael decided to find out about different kinds of banking services.

A **savings account** is a bank account that earns money for you while keeping the money safe.

Interest is the money paid for ucing someone else's money. You can earn interest on money that you save. You pay interest on money that you borrow.

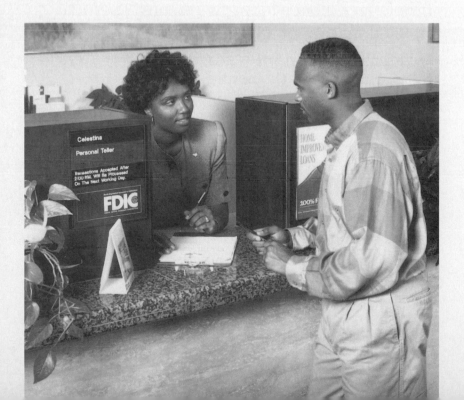

Your money will earn interest in a savings account.

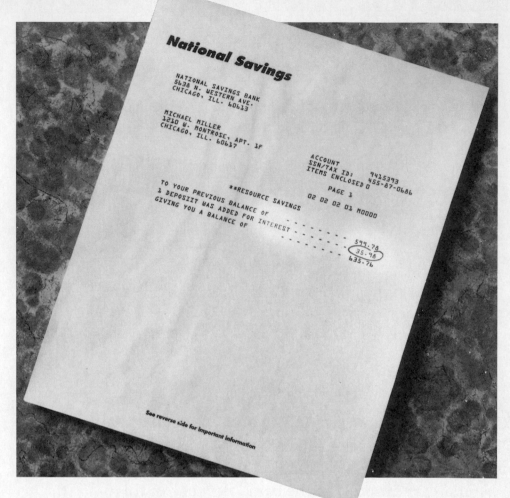

Why Would You Want a Savings Account?

Millions of people save money in bank accounts. People save money for many reasons. They may save to buy a car or a house. They may save for an emergency. Many people save money so they can take vacations. Many people save for their **retirement**.

There are two reasons to put savings in a bank. First, money earns interest in a savings account. Michael put $100 in a savings account. His money earned interest each year. After several years Michael had more than $100. If Michael had kept his savings at home, he would still have only $100 after several years. Second, savings account money cannot be lost or stolen. It is safe because it is protected by the **F.D.I.C.**

Retirement is the period of time when an older person no longer works or when a person leaves a job after many years.

The **F.D.I.C.** is the Federal Deposit Insurance Corporation. This government agency protects the money you have saved in the bank so it will not be lost or stolen.

Banks offer different kinds of savings accounts. Some accounts allow you to **withdraw** your money at any time. Another type of savings account is the **Certificate of Deposit**, or **CD**. Money in these accounts often earns much higher interest. You must leave your money in these accounts for a certain period of time. That period may be six months, one year, two years, or up to five years. Five-year CDs earn higher interest than shorter-term CDs. You lose interest if you withdraw your money before the date the CD allows.

A retirement account is another type of savings account. You can use this account to save a certain amount each year for your retirement. Retirement accounts also help you pay less in taxes. Leave the money in these accounts until you reach age 59½. You lose some of the money if you withdraw it before that age.

To **withdraw** money means to take money out of a bank account.

Banks have machines that allow you to withdraw money from your account when the bank is closed.

Other Banking Services

A **checking account** is a bank account that allows you to take money out of the bank by writing checks.

Banks also offer **checking accounts**. A checking account makes it easier for you to pay bills. You can write checks when you buy goods in stores. You can write checks instead of carrying large amounts of cash with you.

You can also use banks when you need to borrow money. You may need a loan to buy a car. You may need a loan to pay for college or trade or technical school. You pay interest to the bank when you repay your loan.

Banks earn money by charging interest on loans. They use the money in savings accounts to make loans to people. Banks can earn money because they charge much more interest for loans than they pay for money kept in savings accounts.

A **safe deposit box** is a metal box that holds important papers and other items so they cannot be stolen or damaged by fire. It is kept in a bank's vault or safe.

You may have important papers and other items that you want to keep in a safe place. You can rent a **safe deposit box** at a bank to hold your important papers.

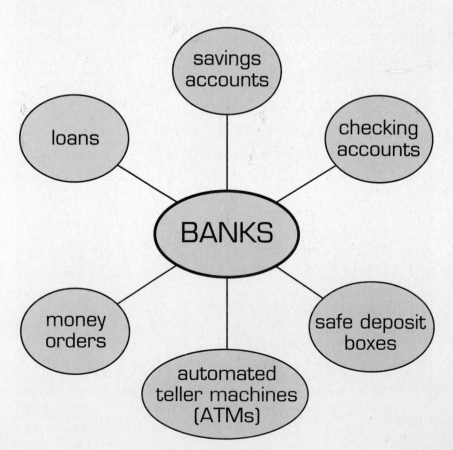

8

Most banks have **automated teller machines**, or **ATMs**. These machines allow you to **deposit** or withdraw money when the bank is closed. You must have a savings or checking account to use the machine. You also need a special card to use the ATM. When you receive your card, ask someone at the bank to show you how to use the machine. Always keep your card in a safe place. Never give your number to anyone else.

Choosing the Right Bank

Not all banks are the same. They pay different amounts of interest for different kinds of accounts. Look for a bank that pays higher interest on savings accounts. You also want a bank that charges less money for other services.

What else do you look for when you choose a bank? You may want a bank that is near your home or your job. You may want a bank that is open on Saturdays. Many banks also stay open late at least one night each week.

Opening a Savings Account

After you choose a bank, you are ready to open an account. A **customer service representative** or bank teller will help you open your account. This person will fill out forms with you. These forms will ask for your name, address, and telephone number. You will need your **social security number** and your date of birth. You need to know the telephone number of the place where you work. You will be asked to use your full name to sign forms. If you are a married woman, you may be asked for your **maiden name**.

You will need two kinds of **identification** in order to open an account. The identification can be a driver's license and a credit card. A photo ID or a passport can also be used. Find out what kind of identification your bank wants.

To **deposit** means to put money into an account.

A **customer service representative** is a worker who helps you use services.

Your **social security number** shows that you are part of the social security system. This system gives money to older people and to the disabled.

A **maiden name** is the family name that a woman used as a child.

Identification is a paper or card that proves who you are.

After you complete the forms, you will be asked to put money in your new account. You will be given your own account number. Use this number every time you deposit money in your account. Use your number every time you withdraw money.

Savings accounts are one type of bank service. Banks provide many different services. These services help you save and borrow money. They allow you to write checks and protect important papers. Visit banks to learn about the services that can help you.

Banks provide many services, including safe deposit boxes.

Completing Deposit and Withdrawal Forms

A deposit form tells the bank to put money into an account. Michael filled out the deposit form below. Notice the following parts.

1 ▶ ◀ **2**

National Savings Bank		Deposit		
Checks and other items are received for deposit subject to the terms and conditions of the bank's account agreement. Deposits may not be available for immediate withdrawal.			Dollars	Cents
		Cash	35	10
		Checks - List Separately 1	25	00
Account Title (Print Name)		2	70	60
Michael Miller		3		
		4		
Deposit To: (Check One)	☑Savings ☐ Checking	5		
		6		
Date	Account Number	7		
1 | 12 | 94	9 4 1 5 3 9 3	Total Deposit	130	70

1 ▶ **Banking Information.** The "account title" is the name of the account's owner. It should be printed.

2 ▶ **Deposit Information.** If you want to deposit cash, write the amount you are putting into the account. If you want to deposit checks, list each check that you are putting into the account. Be sure to **endorse** each check by writing your name on the back of it. Write your name exactly as it appears on the front of the check. Also write your account number on the back of the check. Add all of the money and write the total amount on the deposit form.

▼▼▼

Use Michael's deposit form to answer the following questions.

1. What is the account title on this deposit form? _____

2. What type of account is checked on this form? _____

3. On what date was this form completed? _____

4. What is the account number on this form? _____

5. How much cash is being deposited? _____

6. How many checks are being deposited? _____

A **withdrawal form** tells the bank to take money out of an account. Michael filled out the withdrawal form below. Notice the following parts.

Ⓝ National Savings Bank				Withdrawal
Withdrawal Amount (In Words)	*ninety-two*			Dollars
Date 2	10	94	Signature *Michael Miller*	
Please issue Money Order(s) in the amount(s) of:			Dollars Cents	Below for bank use only. Money Order/Official Check #
			60	00	
		Cash ▶	32	00	No Book ☐
Account Number 9 4 1 5 3 9 3			Total Withdrawal 92	00	Passbook Balance After Update

1 **Banking Information.** Use words to write the total amount you are taking out of your account. Write the date by using numbers. Put the month, day, and year. Sign your name as it appears on your account.

2 **Withdrawal Information.** If you need money orders, list what you need. Write the amount of cash you want to receive. Add the amounts for the money orders and the cash to get the total withdrawal. Use numbers to write the total.

3 The shaded area is for the bank's use. Leave that part blank.

▼ ▼ ▼

Use Michael's withdrawal form to answer the following questions.

1. What is the withdrawal amount in words? _____

2. On what date was this form completed? _____

3. How much did Michael withdraw in a money order? _____

4. How much cash did Michael want? _____

5. What is the account number? _____

6. What is the total withdrawal? _____

WORKSHOP PRACTICE: Complete a Withdrawal Form

Complete the withdrawal form on this page by using the following information. Look back at page 12 if you need help to complete the form.

1. total amount of withdrawal   Eighty-nine

2. date   today's date

3. signature   sign your name

4. money order $61.25

5. cash withdrawal $27.75

6. account number   3256219

7. total withdrawal $89.00

Include all other information that is needed.

N National Savings Bank			**Withdrawal**
Withdrawal Amount (In Words)			Dollars
Date		Signature	
Please issue Money Order(s) in the amount(s) of:		Dollars / Cents	Below for bank use only. Money Order/Official Check #
	Cash ▶		No Book ☐
Account Number		Total Withdrawal	Passbook Balance After Update

 COMPREHENSION: Write the Answer

Write one or more sentences to answer each question.

1. Why do people want to keep their money in a savings account?

_____

_____

2. What are four services that banks offer?

_____

_____

3. How do banks earn money?

_____

_____

4. How do you decide which bank to use?

_____

_____

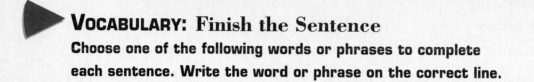

VOCABULARY: Finish the Sentence

Choose one of the following words or phrases to complete each sentence. Write the word or phrase on the correct line.

retirement
withdrawal form
deposit
maiden name
interest
identification

1. When you take money out of your bank account, you

complete a _____ .

2. The money that the bank pays you for keeping your money in a savings account is called

_____ .

3. A woman's family name when she was a child was her

_____ .

4. The time when a person leaves a job after many years

is called _____ .

5. Your driver's license can be used for

_____ because it shows who you are.

6. When you put money into an account, you

_____ it.

THINKING AND WRITING Banks offer many different services. Which services would be most helpful to you now? Which services do you think you might need at some other time? Explain in your journal.

USING A CHECKING ACCOUNT

Think About As You Read

▶ Why would you want to use a checking account?

▶ How do you keep records for your checking account?

Maria felt proud of her new apartment. She enjoyed having her own place. But she now had more bills to pay. Maria decided it would be easier to pay bills if she had her own checking account.

Why Use a Checking Account?

There are five reasons to use a checking account.

1. You can use your checking account to cash your paycheck. Or you can deposit your paycheck into your checking account. Then you can write checks with the money in your checking account.

Your bank can offer you several kinds of checking accounts.

15

2. You can use checks to pay bills by mail. Never mail cash. Cash can be stolen in the mail.

3. It is safer to use checks than to use cash. If your check is lost or stolen, you can ask your bank to **stop payment** on the check. Then you do not lose the money shown on the check. The bank will charge you for a stop payment request.

4. It is often cheaper to have a checking account than to buy money orders. You pay extra for every money order.

5. A checking account helps you keep a record of how you use your money. Your bank will return **canceled checks** or a list of canceled checks to you. Keep these checks. They show how you spent your money.

You can use checks to make purchases.

Checks come in many different styles.

Opening a Checking Account

You may want to keep your savings account and your checking account in the same bank. Then you can **transfer**, or move, your money from savings to checking when you need to write checks. You can earn interest on the money while it is in the savings account.

You can choose the kind of checking account you use. Think about the number of checks you may write each month. If you will write many checks, you may need to keep a large balance in your account. A free checking account would be good for you. You do not pay a **fee** for this kind of account if you keep a **minimum balance** in your checking account at all times. The bank may charge a fee ($4 to $15) for each month that your balance is too low.

If you will not write many checks, you may not need to keep a large balance in your account. So you may want a **budget checking account**. With this

A **fee** is the money charged for a service.

Your checking account **balance** is the amount of money you have in your account. If your bank requires a **minimum balance** then your account cannot go below a certain amount.

A **budget checking account** is a low-cost checking account. It is good for people who write only a few checks each month.

17

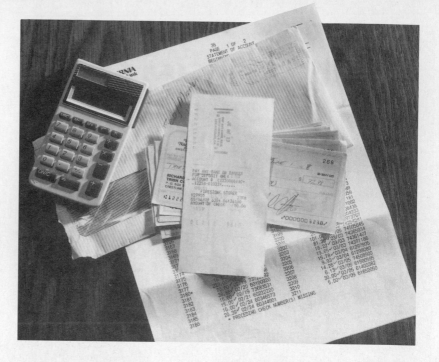

account, you pay a small fee each month. You also pay about 25 cents for each check you write. The bank takes money from your checking account to pay these fees.

To open a checking account, you will be asked to fill out forms. These forms are very much like the ones used to open savings accounts. You may need two kinds of identification to open your checking account.

The bank needs a record of your signature. So you will be asked to sign signature cards. Decide if your name will be the only one on your checking account. You may want a **joint checking account**. Then the names of both account owners are printed on the checks. Both owners can write checks.

Your bank will have checks and deposit slips printed for you. Or you can order them yourself. Your checks will have your name, address, and account number on them. You will have to pay for the checks and deposit slips made for your account.

Using Your Checking Account

Keep good records for your checking account. To do this, use a **checkbook register**. Use the register to

A **joint checking account** is a bank account that belongs to two people.

A **checkbook register** is a book that is used to keep a record of all the checks and deposits of a checking account.

write down all deposits. Add all deposits to your balance. Also record the date, number, **payee**, and amount of every check that you write. Subtract every check that you write from the balance.

> Each time you write a check, the bank withdraws the amount of money on the check from your checking account. What happens if you do not have enough money in your account to cover a check you write? The bank marks the check **insufficient funds**. The check is returned to the payee. A returned check is called an **overdraft**. The bank will charge you a fee ($10 to $20) for each overdraft. If you write a check for more than you have in your account, your account will be **overdrawn**. The bank will charge you every time you overdraw your account.

Be careful with your checking account. A checking account can help you. You can write checks to pay bills instead of buying money orders or paying cash. But remember to record all your checks and deposits. Know how much money is in your account before you write checks. Keep good records and check your account each month so you know how much money you have.

A **payee** is the person or company to whom a check is written.

If you have **insufficient funds** you do not have enough money in your bank account to cover your checks.

An **overdraft** occurs when you write a check for more money than you have in your checking account.

Your account is **overdrawn** when you do not have enough money in your account to cover your checks.

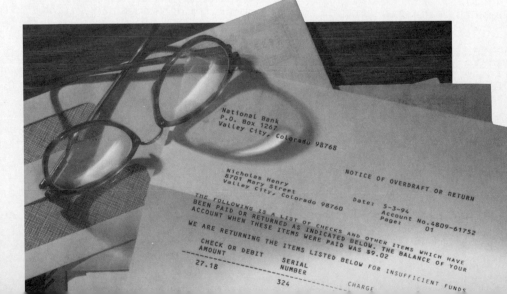

The bank will charge you extra if you overdraw your account.

19

Writing a Check

Here is a check that Maria wrote. Notice the following parts.

```
Maria Sanchez                                        103
30 Bear Street
Phoenix, Arizona 35034          1-27  19 94   1-7012-2280    ▸1

Pay to the order of  Marcy's Department Store        $ 21.76
Twenty-one and 76/100 ～～～～～～～～～～        Dollars   ▸2

◖National Savings Bank

For  sweater                        Maria Sanchez            ▸3

⑆226070128⑆ 103 ⑈0100105493
```

1 ▸ **When.** The date can be written by using words or numbers.

2 ▸ **How Much.** The amount of money is first written by using numbers. Write close to the dollar sign. Use a decimal point to separate dollars and cents. On the next line, use words to write the same amount of money. Start writing the amount at the beginning of the line. Write the dollar amount in words. Then write "and." Write the cents as a fraction of a dollar, such as 76/100. Draw a wavy line across the empty space on this line. Do this so no one can change the amount of the check.

3 ▸ **Signature.** Sign your name as it is on your signature card.

▼ ▼ ▼

Use Maria's check to answer the following questions.

1. When did Maria write this check? _____

2. Who is Maria paying with this check? _____

3. What is the amount of money on this check? Write the amount in both numbers and words. _____

_____

4. What did Maria buy with this check? _____

Here is Maria's checkbook register. Notice the following parts.

①		②	③			④	⑤	
Item No. or Trans. Code	Date	TRANSACTION DESCRIPTION	Subtractions Amount of Payment or Withdrawal (−)	✓ T	(−) Fee if Any	Additions Amount of Deposit or Interest (+)	Balance	
	1/17	*Built Well Company* *paycheck*				300 00	300 00	— balance
101	1/24	*Major Telephone* *monthly bill*	26 30				−26 30 273 70	— balance
102	1/26	*Apartment City* *rent*	205 00				−205 00 68 70	— balance
	1/27	*M. R. Smith* *refund*				150 00	+150 00 218 70	— balance
103	1/27	*Marcy's Department Store* *sweater*	21 76				−21 76 196 94	— balance
								— balance

 Item Number or Transaction Code. Record the check number.

 Transaction Description. This space is to record whom you write a check to or receive a deposit from. The shaded area can be used to make a note about the check or deposit.

▶ **Subtractions.** This space is to write the amount of a check. It will be subtracted from the account balance.

▶ **Additions.** This space is to write the amount of a deposit. It will be added to the account balance.

▶ **Balance.** This space is to write the amount of the balance after each deposit is added and each check is subtracted.

▼ ▼ ▼

Use Maria's checkbook register to answer the following questions.

1. On what date did Maria first make a deposit? _____

2. What was Maria's first balance? _____

3. What was the number of the check Maria wrote to pay her rent? _____

4. How much did Maria pay to Apartment City? _____

5. How much did Maria deposit on January 27? _____

21

Reading a Bank Statement

Each month you will receive a bank statement that tells your account balance. You may receive the canceled checks and a list of your deposits and withdrawals. Use the statement to balance your checkbook. You may need to list bank fees in your checkbook to get your account to balance. Be sure your checkbook amount matches the bank statement. If it does not, check with the bank.

Maria's bank statement is on the next page. Notice the following parts.

 Account Summary. This area gives the previous balance. It tells how much money was put into the account and how much money was taken out of the account. **Debits** are charges that were subtracted from the account. This area also gives the current balance.

 Deposits and Credits. This area lists all money put into the account.

 Checks and Debits. This area lists all money taken out of the account. The date of the check on the bank statement is the date that it cleared the bank, not the date that it was written.

▼ ▼ ▼

Use Maria's bank statement to answer the following questions.

1. What is Maria's current balance on this statement? _____

2. What was Maria's previous balance? _____

3. How many deposits and credits are on this statement? _____

4. How many checks and debits are on this statement? _____

5. What is the date of this statement? _____

6. On what date did check number 103 clear the bank? _____

7. Balance Maria's checkbook. Find the deposits and the checks listed on the bank statement. Put a check mark by them in the √ column on Maria's checkbook register on page 21.

8. One listing is not in Maria's checkbook register. The bank subtracted $12.00 from Maria's account to pay for her checks. Write this information in Maria's checkbook register. Subtract $12.00 from her balance in the register. Does the balance in her checkbook register match the balance on the bank statement? _____ What is it? _____

National Savings Bank   STATEMENT

MARIA SANCHEZ   DATE 1-31-94
30 BEAR STREET   ACCOUNT 0100105493
PHOENIX, ARIZONA 35034

ACCOUNT NO. 0100105493   NEW CHECKING
PREVIOUS BALANCE   0.00
 2 DEPOSITS AND CREDITS   450.00
 4 CHECKS AND DEBITS   265.06
CURRENT BALANCE   184.94

DEPOSITS AND CREDITS

DATE	AMOUNT	DESCRIPTION
1-17	300.00	DEPOSIT
1-27	150.00	DEPOSIT

CHECKS AND DEBITS

DATE	NUMBER/DESCRIPTION	AMOUNT
1-21	CHECK ORDER	12.00
1-27	101	26.30
1-30	102	205.00
1-30	103	21.76

WORKSHOP PRACTICE: Write a Check

Write your own check. Use check number 224 below. Make the check out to Smith's Store for $11.99 to pay for food. Use today's date and sign your name. Look back at the check on page 20 if you need help.

		224
	19	1-7012-2280

Pay to the order of _____ $ _____

_____ Dollars

Ⓝ National Savings Bank

For _____

⑆246⑈81012 224 0100105217

In the register below write the check number, date, payee, and amount of the check you just wrote. Also write what the check is for. Subtract the check from the balance. Circle the new balance.

Item No. or Trans. Code	Date	TRANSACTION DESCRIPTION	Subtractions Amount of Payment or Withdrawal (–)		✔ T	(–) Fee if Any	Additions Amount of Deposit or Interest (+)	Balance
223	2/7	Department of Public Safety license renewal	10	00				250 00
								–10 00
								240 00

VOCABULARY: Find the Meaning

On the line write the word or phrase that best completes each sentence.

1. The money that you pay for a service is a _____ .

signature   account   fee

2. The amount of money in your checking account is your

_____ .

tax   balance   withdrawal

3. The way you sign your name is your _____ .

signature   account   register

4. The bank has withdrawn money to pay for a _____ .

canceled check   balance   deposit

COMPREHENSION: True or False

Write True next to each sentence that is true. Write False next to each sentence that is false. There are two false sentences.

_____ **1.** It is safe to mail cash.

_____ **2.** All checking accounts are the same.

_____ **3.** You should subtract each check that you write from your checkbook balance.

_____ **4.** You should record every check you write in your checkbook register.

On the lines that follow, rewrite the two false sentences to make them true.

_____

_____

THINKING AND WRITING If you ever write an overdraft on your checking account, what do you think you should do? Explain your answer in your journal.

CREDIT AND INTEREST

Think About As You Read

▶ How can you use credit cards safely?

▶ What should you do if your credit card is stolen?

▶ What forms of credit can be used to buy expensive products?

Ramon needs a new refrigerator. The one he wants to buy costs $550. Ramon saves $30 from his paycheck each week. But it will take him more than four months to save enough money for the refrigerator. Ramon cannot wait that long. So he will buy the refrigerator by using **credit**. He will have the new refrigerator in a few days.

Buying with **credit** means borrowing money to buy goods now and pay for them later.

Credit can help you buy expensive products.

Many companies offer credit card services.

Understanding Credit

Credit allows you to buy goods and services and pay for them at a later time. When you use credit to buy goods, you are really borrowing money. You are borrowing from a store, bank, or credit company. Stores, banks, and credit companies often charge interest for goods bought with credit. Interest makes goods cost more. So most goods cost more money when they are bought with credit.

Understanding Credit Cards

One way to buy on credit is to use **credit cards**. Credit cards allow you to buy goods and pay for them at a later date.

There are different kinds of credit cards. Some credit cards are called **major credit cards.** A major credit card can be used in thousands of different stores. You can get major credit cards through banks.

Credit cards are cards that let you buy goods and pay for them after you get the bill.

Major credit cards are prepared by banks and can be used in many different businesses.

Credit cards can make shopping easier.

An **application** is a written form you fill out to apply for something, such as a credit card.

Many large stores have their own credit cards. These cards can only be used in different branches of the same store.

How can you get a credit card? You must be eighteen years old. First, fill out a credit card **application**. The Life Skills Workshop on page 32 shows you how to do this. After you have filled out the application, mail it to the address on the form. Then wait a few weeks. During that time the credit card company will check the information on your application. The company wants to be sure you will be able to pay your credit card bills.

There are four reasons to use credit cards. First, credit cards can be used instead of money. So you can carry less money with you when you shop. Second, you have fewer bills to pay. You can buy goods in different stores with the same major credit card. At the end of the month, you will receive one bill for all the goods you bought with your credit card. Third, you can use your major credit card when you are traveling. Your card can be used in stores and hotels around the world. The fourth reason to use credit cards is to build a good **credit rating**. If you always pay your bills on time, you will have a good credit rating. A good credit rating makes it easier to get a loan from a bank. If you have a good credit rating, you may pay less interest on loans.

Your **credit rating** tells whether or not you are able to pay back the money you have borrowed.

It is easy to have **debt** problems because of credit cards. If you use your cards to buy more than you can afford, you cannot pay your monthly bills. Credit card companies allow you to pay a small part of your bill each month. But they charge very high interest on the part of the bill you cannot pay. You can develop a very large debt with credit cards.

A **debt** is money that has been borrowed from a person or business.

Using Credit Cards Safely

Use your credit cards carefully. Then they will not become a problem for you. One way you can prevent problems is to pay your bills on time.

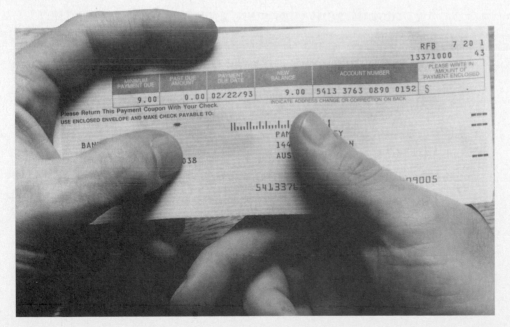

Pay your credit card bills on time so you will not be charged interest.

The **due date** is the day that your payment for a credit card bill must be received by the company.

The **minimum payment** is the least amount you can pay. It is listed on the credit card bill.

An **installment plan** allows you to buy a product and pay for it in monthly payments with interest.

A **down payment** is the first payment for a product bought with credit. A down payment pays only part of the cost of the product.

Every credit card bill has a **due date**. Pay the full amount by the due date. If you cannot pay the full amount, pay the **minimum payment** due. You will be charged interest on the amount you do not pay.

What should you do if your credit card is lost or stolen? You want to stop a thief from using your credit card. Keep a record of your credit card number. Call the credit office at the bank or store that gave you the card. Tell the customer service representative that your card was lost or stolen. Report the account number on your credit card. The store or bank will close your account for a few weeks. No one will be able to use your credit card. A new card will be sent to you. The new card will have a different account number.

You will receive a credit card statement each month. Your statement will list all the products you bought with your card. Your statement will tell you how much money to pay. Always check your statement. Look for mistakes. Did you really buy everything on your statement? Are the prices what you paid? Call the credit card company if you think there is a mistake on your bill.

Other Kinds of Credit

Installment plans are another form of credit. With these plans, you make a **down payment** to a store to buy a product. Then you pay the store a part of the cost each month. You also pay an interest charge each month.

You can use installment plans to buy products for your home. After you make the down payment, you can take your products home. The products will cost you more than the selling price because of the interest charges.

Loans are another kind of credit. You can borrow money to buy very expensive products. You may take out a loan to buy a car or furniture. Each month

Some stores offer installment plans to help you buy products.

you repay part of the loan with interest. Banks and credit unions often make loans.

Use credit carefully. Never borrow more money than you can repay. It is against the law to borrow money and not repay it.

Credit can help you get the things you need. It can also help you buy some of the things you want. Use credit to buy only what you can afford. Pay your bills on time. Then you will be using credit to improve the way you live.

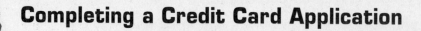

LIFE SKILLS Workshop

Completing a Credit Card Application

Look at the sample credit card application on page 33. It was filled out by Ramon. Notice the following parts.

 Personal Information. This part asks for the length of time you lived at each address. The credit card company is looking for **stability**, or how long you stay in one place.

 Job Information. Your **position** means the kind of work you do. The credit card company wants to know if you have a job.

 Income. This credit card company requires a person to have a total income of $12,000. Other companies may require different amounts. Your **annual salary** is the money you earn each year from your job. Other **yearly income** includes all the other money you get each year. Savings account interest is part of your income.

 Accounts. You can find your account numbers printed on your checks and deposit slips.

 Signature. When you sign your name, it means you understand and agree with the terms given on the form. You are allowing the credit card company to check into your background. The company will check to see if you have a job, how much you earn, and if you pay your bills.

▼ ▼ ▼

Use Ramon's application to answer the following questions.

1. How long has Ramon lived at his current address? _____

2. What is Ramon's birth date? _____

3. Who is Ramon's employer? _____

4. What is Ramon's position? _____

5. What is Ramon's total income? _____

6. Does Ramon have any credit cards? _____

DOLLARMASTER CREDIT CARD APPLICATION

Print clearly in ink.
Fill out this simple application form in full.
Print your name as you would like it
to appear on your card.

DOLLARMA$TER

1 PERSONAL INFORMATION

	First	Middle	Last
Your Name	Ramon	Jorge	Ortega

Your Home Address (Number and Street) **20 Lincoln Street**   Apt. No.

City or Town **Lakewood**   State **N.J.**   Zip Code **08701**

How Many Years Have You Lived Here? **2**

Do You (check one):
☑ Own Your Home   ☐ Rent   Other:
☐ Own Your Condo/Co-op   ☐ Live with Parents

Date of Birth	Month	Day	Year	Home Phone Number (include area code)	Social Security Number
	0 6	0 2	6 6	(908) 305-2219	311-92-0237

Where Did You Live Before This?

Address **99 Elm Street**   Apt. No.   How Many Years Did You Live There? **8**

City or Town **Lakewood**   State **N.J.**   Zip Code **08701**

Are You a Permanent U.S. Resident?
☑ Yes   ☐ No

2 JOB INFORMATION

Your Employer (Business Name) **Greenway Builders**

Position **Construction Worker**   How Long Have You Worked Here? **2 years**

Work Phone Number (include area code) **(908) 305-6600**

Check Here If You Are: ☐ Retired   ☐ Self-Employed
If retired or self-employed, please complete the following information:

Bank Name:

Bank Phone Number (include area code) **( )**   Bank Account #

3 INCOME

Your total income from all sources must be at least $12,000 a year to be considered for cardmembership.

Your Annual Salary **$ 23,500**

Other Yearly Income **$85**

Source of Other Income **bank interest**

4 ACCOUNTS

Please check all those that apply. Be sure to write in the name of the bank.

☑ Checking Account # **300216531**   Bank: (Name) **National Savings**

☑ Savings Account # **3924716**   Bank: (Name) **National Savings**

☐ Visa/MasterCard   ☐ Diner's Club   ☐ American Express
☐ Department Store   ☑ Gasoline   ☐ Other

5 PLEASE SIGN THIS AUTHORIZATION

I have read and understood both sides of this application and I agree to the terms and conditions as described on the back of this application.

X **Ramon Ortega**   **9-12-94**
APPLICANT'S SIGNATURE   DATE

33

Check Your Skills

▶ **WORKSHOP PRACTICE: Complete a Credit Card Application**

You may decide to get a credit card. You will need to fill out
an application. Part of an application is on this page. Fill in
all the information. Look back at the application on page 33
if you are unsure about what to do.

DOLLARMASTER CREDIT CARD APPLICATION

Print clearly in ink.
Fill out this simple application form in full.
Print your name as you would like it
  to appear on your card.

PERSONAL INFORMATION

	First	Middle	Last

Your
Name

Your Home Address
(Number and Street) .... Apt. No.

City or Town ...... State ...... Zip Code

How Many Years
Have You
Lived Here?

Do You (check one):
☐ Own Your Home   ☐ Rent   Other:
☐ Own Your Condo/Co-op ☐ Live with Parents

Date of Birth | Month | Day | Year   Home Phone Number (include area code) ( )   Social Security Number

Where Did You Live Before This?

Address ...... Apt. No. ...... How Many Years Did You Live There?

City or Town ...... State ...... Zip Code

Are You a Permanent U. S. Resident?
☐ Yes   ☐ No

JOB INFORMATION

Your Employer (Business Name)

Position   How Long Have You Worked Here?

Work Phone Number (include area code) ( )

Check Here If You Are: ☐ Retired ☐ Self-Employed
If retired or self-employed, please complete the following information:

Bank Name:

Bank Phone Number (include area code) ( )   Bank Account #

INCOME

Your total income from all sources must be at least $12,000 a year to be considered for cardmembership.

Your Annual Salary $ _____

Other Yearly Income

Source of Other Income

ACCOUNTS

Please check all those that apply. Be sure to write in the name of the bank.

☐ Checking Account #   Bank: (Name)

☐ Savings Account #   Bank: (Name)

☐ Visa/MasterCard   ☐ Diner's Club   ☐ American Express
☐ Department Store   ☐ Gasoline   ☐ Other

34

VOCABULARY: Writing with Vocabulary Words

Use five or more of the following words or phrases to write a paragraph that tells about credit and interest.

credit
credit cards
application
major credit card
due date
installment plan
down payment
credit rating

_____

_____

_____

_____

_____

_____

_____

COMPREHENSION: Finish the Paragraph

Use the following words to finish the paragraph. Write the words you choose on the correct lines.

credit
installment plan
loan
interest
debt
major credit card

When you buy a product and pay for it at a later time, you are using _____ . You can buy goods in many different stores and be billed for all of them together by using a _____ . If you cannot pay all of your credit card bills, the credit card company will charge you high _____ . If you use your credit cards to buy more than you can afford, you will have _____ problems. There are other ways to buy products and pay for them later. You can use an _____ or get a _____ to buy very expensive goods.

 **THINKING AND WRITING** What kind of credit do you think you might need? How will you be able to avoid having debt problems? Explain your ideas in your journal.

PLANNING YOUR BUDGET

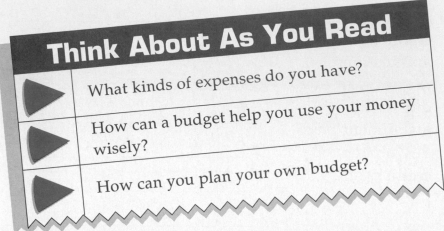

Think About As You Read

▶ What kinds of expenses do you have?

▶ How can a budget help you use your money wisely?

▶ How can you plan your own budget?

Yoshi has just started a new job. Her take-home pay will be $800 each month. She will have $200 to spend each week. She must use that money to pay for rent, food, and all her needs. Yoshi worries about having enough money to pay for everything she needs. Yoshi needs a plan for spending and saving money. That plan will be her **budget**.

Understanding Your Income and Expenses

Your income is all the money you earn during a period of time. You earn money from your job. The interest you get from your savings adds to your income.

A **budget** is a plan for spending money and for saving money. With a good budget, you spend less than you make.

Your paycheck will have to cover all your bills.

Include money for needs like food in your budget.

Most people have a **fixed income**. They earn the same amount of money at their job every month. The amount changes when they get a raise.

You use your income to pay your **expenses**. You have two kinds of expenses. They are your needs and your wants. You need food, clothes, and a home. Your wants help you enjoy life. You may want to go out to eat. You may want to go to concerts and movies.

Expenses are all the things you pay money for.

Your budget helps you plan how to spend and save your money. Your budget includes all of your needs. It includes some of the things you want. Your budget can also help you save some money each month.

Planning Your Own Budget

Plan your budget so your income will be greater than the money you spend. Some people spend more money than they earn. They must borrow money to pay their expenses. Before long, these people have large debts.

Find ways to cut expenses. Cut down on heat and air conditioning.

Renter's insurance protects you if you rent an apartment. If your apartment is robbed, you will receive money for your losses.

Before you plan a budget, you need to know how you spend your money. Write down all of your expenses for a few weeks. Look for ways that you can spend less money. Perhaps you can spend less on food by buying fewer snacks. Perhaps you can spend less on electricity by turning down the heat.

Include a plan for large expenses in your budget. For example, perhaps your rent is $400 a month. You will need to save $100 each week to have the money you need for rent. Perhaps once a year you must pay $150 for **renter's insurance** for your apartment. If you save $12.50 every month, you will be able to pay the $150 bill once a year. By saving $3 each week, you would also have $150 to pay your insurance bill.

You can plan a monthly budget. To do this, follow this six-step plan.

1. List all your needs.

2. List some of your wants.

3. Add your needs and wants to get your total expenses.

4. Write down your monthly income.

5. Subtract your expenses from your income.

6. The money you have left will be your savings.

Monthly Budget

1. Needs	$585
2. Wants	+200
3. Total expenses	$785
4. Monthly income	$850
5. Subtract expenses	−785
6. Your savings	$65

Planning a Budget That Works

Yoshi planned her first budget. It is on page 40. She wrote down all her needs and wants. Then she saw that she was spending more money than she earned. So she planned a different budget. She would save money by renting a cheaper apartment. She would save more money by not buying a car and not getting cable TV. The second budget allowed Yoshi to pay for all her expenses. It also allowed her to save more money each month. Yoshi decided to use the second budget.

Include all your expenses when you plan your budget.

First Budget

Needs
rent	$ 320
telephone	20
electricity	20
gas	10
food	160
renter's insurance	12.50
medical	40
laundry	30
new clothes	40
car payment	100
car insurance	75
car expenses	60

Wants
cable TV	$ 30
restaurant	30
movies	20
hobby	25
extras	30

Total expenses $ 1022.50

Monthly income $ 800.00
subtract expenses - 1022.50

Debt $ -222.50

Second Budget

Needs
rent	$ 250
telephone	20
electricity	20
gas	10
food	160
renter's insurance	12.50
medical	40
laundry	30
new clothes	40
bus to work	72

Wants
restaurant	$ 30
movies	20
hobby	25
extras	30

Total expenses $ 759.50

Monthly income $ 800.00
subtract expenses - 759.50

Savings $ 40.50

Sometimes your budget will change. It will change when your income changes. It will change when your needs and wants change. If you buy a car, your budget will change to help you pay for the car.

A good budget will help you pay for your needs and wants. It will also help you save money each month. Try not to spend more money each month than your budget allows. By living with your budget, you will be able to save money for your future.

LIFE SKILLS Workshop

Planning Your Own Monthly Budget

Plan a budget that will help you handle your expenses for a month. Your goal is to spend less than you earn. Then you will be able to put money in your savings account.

▶ **STEP 1.** Add all the money you earn each month to get your total monthly income.

Income from work _____

Other income _____

Total monthly income _____

▶ **STEP 2.** List all of your needs and how much they cost each month. Add your own special needs to the list.

NEED	COST
rent or house payment	_____
telephone	_____
electricity	_____
gas	_____
food	_____
transportation	_____
insurance	_____
medical care	_____
laundry	_____
new clothes	_____
_____	_____
_____	_____
Total Needs	_____

Check your bills to see if you are staying within your budget.

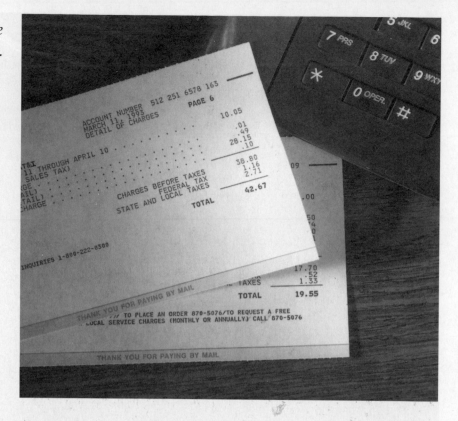

Some bills help you learn how you are using company services. For example, you may receive a very large phone bill. Look at smaller bills from past months. Check to see if you have been making many more calls. Then you can lower your next bill by making fewer calls.

Paying Bills by Mail

Many companies send bills in the mail. It is not hard to pay bills by mail. You can pay your bill when you get it. Or you can wait until closer to the due date. If you miss the due date, you may have to pay extra.

Follow these six steps to pay your bills by mail.

1. Write a check for the amount of the bill.

2. Record the check in your checkbook register.

3. Write your billing account number on your check.

4. Put your check and your bill in an envelope.

Sometimes you mail only one part of the bill. You keep the other part. Many bills come with their own envelopes. Some envelopes have windows. Make sure the mailing address can be seen in the envelope window.

5. Put a stamp on the envelope. Write your return address.

6. Mail the bill a few days before its due date. Some bills may tell you to mail the payment at least five days before the due date. That is to make sure the company gets the payment on time.

Paying bills on time is a good habit. Paying your bills and staying out of debt will help you build a good credit rating. Compare your bills and your budget to see if you are spending your money as planned.

Include your billing account number on your check when you pay a bill.

Paying a Credit Card Bill

Jason Porter received a credit card bill from Lang's Department Store. The bill is on the next page. Study the bill to understand how to pay credit card bills.

1 **Payment Information.** The top portion of the statement is the part that you tear off and return with your payment. It tells the due date. The payment must be received by this date. The bill **closing date** is the last day of the billing period. Anything bought after this date will be on the next bill. The total amount due is the amount you owe on this credit card account. The minimum payment is the smallest amount of money you are allowed to pay. If you pay only the minimum, a finance charge will be added to the next bill. If you pay the full amount, you will not be charged interest.

2 **Purchases Made.** This section lists everything that was bought with the card during the billing period.

3 **Account Summary.** The previous balance is the amount that was due during the last billing period. The total payments have already been made. The annual percentage rate is the interest that is charged for credit.

▼ ▼ ▼

Use Jason's credit card bill to answer the following questions.

1. What is the due date of this bill? _____

2. What is the total amount due on this bill? _____

3. What is the minimum payment due on this bill? _____

4. What amount is Jason paying? _____

5. How many purchases did Jason make? _____

6. What was Jason's previous balance? _____

7. What amount did Jason pay on his last bill? _____

8. What is the yearly interest rate? _____

LANG'S

CUSTOMER STATEMENT

MAR. 15, 1994	BILL CLOSING DATE	ACCOUNT NUMBER
	2/18/94	270-776-41

TOTAL AMOUNT DUE IF PAYMENT RECEIVED BY DUE DATE	MINIMUM PAYMENT NOW DUE	Please Indicate Amount Paid
58.97	20.00	58.97

◣ 1

JASON R. PORTER
4 OCEAN DRIVE
SAN DIEGO, CA 92109

IF ADDRESS IS WRONG, PLEASE CORRECT

ADDRESS _____

CITY _____

STATE _____ ZIP _____

TELEPHONE NO. _____

AREA CODE ( )

|..ll..ll..lll..l.l.l..ll...ll..lll..ll..l.l..|

270 776 41 00164390002000

- -

PLEASE RETURN TOP PORTION OF
STATEMENT WITH YOUR PAYMENT

DATE	STORE	REFERENCE NO.	DEPT.	TRANSACTION DESCRIPTION	CHARGES	PAYMENTS & CREDITS
2/09	26	08500015	572	YOUNG MEN'S KNITS/SWEATER	19.99	
2/09	26	08577240	309	SPORTING GOODS	31.99	
2/09	26	08126674	451	MEN'S SOCKS	6.99	

◣ 2

IT'S EASIER THAN EVER TO PAY YOUR LANG'S CHARGE.
LANG'S CHARGE ACCOUNT PAYMENTS WILL BE ACCEPTED
AT ANY SALES DESK IN ANY LANG'S STORE.

PREVIOUS BALANCE	TOTAL PURCHASES & OTHER CHARGES	TOTAL CREDITS	TOTAL PAYMENTS	FINANCE CHARGE	THIS IS YOUR NEW BALANCE	MINIMUM PAYMENT NOW DUE
89.00	58.97		89.00		58.97	20.00

◣ 3

AVERAGE DAILY BALANCE	PERIODIC RATE	ANNUAL PERCENTAGE RATE	ACCOUNT NUMBER	TYPE	BILL CLOSING DATE	PAYMENT DUE DATE
	1.8	21.6	270-776-41	REGULAR	2/18/94	3/15/94

CREDIT LINE $1000 - AVAILABLE CREDIT $940
BILLING INQUIRIES, 1-800-678-8718 (TOLL FREE)

FOR BILLING INQUIRIES OR TO REPORT A LOST OR
STOLEN CHARGE CARD CALL THE NUMBER LISTED ABOVE

Check Your Skills

WORKSHOP PRACTICE: Read a Credit Card Statement

Read the top part of the credit card statement on this page.
Then answer the questions about the bill.

Make check payable to: **Dollarmaster Card**

Account Number	Payment Due By	New Balance	Minimum Payment	Enter Amount Paid
5396 9141 0129 2972	Feb. 15, 1994	$48.86	15.00	$ *48.86*

Please detatch and return this coupon
with your payment.

Make changes to address and phone number below:

Address

Alison Johnson
305 Park Street
Miami, FL 33156

City   State   Zip

Home phone   Business phone
(   )   (   )

Dollarmaster Card
P.O. Box 1010
Columbus, GA. 31997-0001

DOLLARMA$TER

5396 9141 0129 2972

1. What is Alison's account number? _____

2. By what date must this bill be paid? _____

3. What is the total amount of this bill? _____

4. What is the smallest amount Alison can pay? _____

5. Did Alison decide to pay the full amount?   yes _____   no _____

6. Who should Alison make her check payable to ? _____
_____

VOCABULARY: FIND THE MEANING

On the line write the word or phrase that best completes each sentence.

1. People who lose their jobs have _____ .

     identification   applications   hardships

2. The last day that charges can be added to your account during a billing

   period is the _____ .

     opening date   due date   closing date

3. Pay your bills by the _____ .

closing date   billing period   due date

4. An interest charge that is added to a credit card bill is called a

_____ .

finance charge   fee   tax

5. A credit card bill allows you to pay only a small amount or a

_____ .

insurance   minimum   withdraw

COMPREHENSION: True or False

Write True next to each sentence that is true. Write False next to each sentence that is false. There are two false sentences.

_____ **1.** A finance charge is added to every credit card bill.

_____ **2.** Your telephone and electricity can be turned off if you do not pay your bills.

_____ **3.** When writing a check to pay a bill, you should write your billing account number on the check.

_____ **4.** When paying credit card bills, it is best to pay the minimum.

On the lines that follow, rewrite the two false sentences to make them true.

_____

_____

_____

_____

THINKING AND WRITING Imagine that you did not allow enough money in your budget to pay your electric bill and your phone bill. It is now very hard for you to pay these bills. You do not want to lose these services. In your journal explain how you would handle these problems.

53

CROSSWORD PUZZLE: Money Matters

Use the clues to complete the crossword puzzle.
Choose from the following words.

budget
credit
debt
finance
identification
interest
rating
withdraw

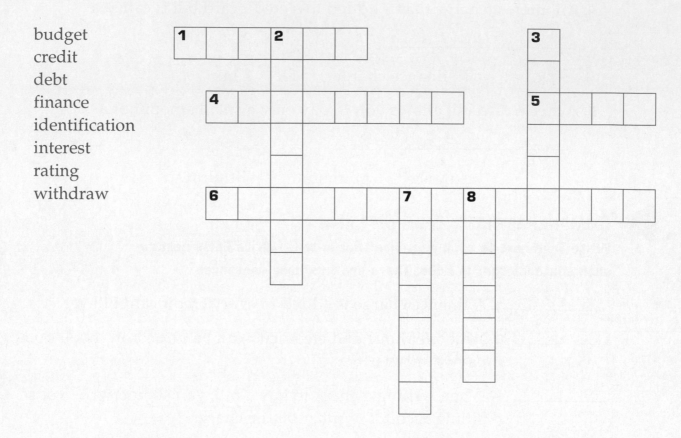

Across

1. Your credit _ _ _ _ _ tells how well you are able to pay back the money you have borrowed.

4. To _ _ _ _ money means to take money out of a bank account.

5. A _ _ _ _ _ is money that is owed to a person or business.

6. _ _ _ _ _ is a paper or card that can be used to prove who you are.

Down

2. _ _ _ _ _ is the money paid for using someone else's money.

3. A _ _ _ _ _ is a plan for spending money and for saving money.

7. A _ _ _ _ _ charge is added to a credit card bill when you do not pay the full balance due.

8. Buying with _ _ _ _ _ means borrowing money to buy goods now and pay for them later.

BEING A SMART SHOPPER

Think About As You Read

▶ How can you save money when buying food?

▶ Why is it important to read clothing labels?

▶ How can you save money when you buy appliances?

Roberto needed a new jacket. He went shopping and saw a jacket that he liked. It cost more than his budget allowed. So Roberto decided to wait. A few weeks later, Roberto found the same jacket in a different store. The price was lower. Roberto bought the jacket. He was proud of himself for being a smart shopper.

Look for sales when you shop.

55

Making Decisions When Shopping

When you shop, you want to get as much as you can for your money. To use your money wisely, ask yourself these questions when you shop.

1. Do I really need this product now?

2. Do I have enough money in my budget to buy this product?

3. Do I need to buy this product with credit? Will I have debts to repay?

4. Could I save money by waiting for a sale?

5. Would this product cost less in another store?

6. Am I buying this product only to **impress** others?

Your job and your income **influence** what you buy. Your job helps you decide what kind of clothes you need for work. A person who works outdoors needs different clothing from an office worker.

To **impress** means to affect the way others think and feel.

To **influence** means to change the ideas and actions of others.

Check the newspaper for sale ads when you need to buy a product.

56

3.

4.

5.

Beir

V
mon
the l
thos

T
label
label
wate
swea
wash

Check your grocery list, ads, and coupons before you go shopping.

Advertisements, or ads, try to influence you to buy products. Ads give you information about different kinds of products. Many companies spend a great deal of money for ads on TV. Do not buy a product just because of the ads. Make sure the product is really a good buy. Check newspaper ads for prices. Ads can tell you when products are on sale.

Being a Smart Food Shopper

Food may be a large part of your budget. A shopping list can help you use your food budget wisely. Keep a list in your kitchen. Write down the foods you need during the week. Check your list before going to the store. When you get to the store, buy foods that are on your list. Avoid buying other foods that you want but do not need.

Comparison shopping can help you save money. To comparison shop you compare prices. Compare the price of the same food in different stores. Compare the price of one **brand** with another. Try to buy the brand with the lowest price. For example, one brand of orange juice may cost much less than another. You may want to buy the cheaper brand.

Advertisements are ads. Ads try to make you want to buy a product. Ads tell you what is special about a product.

Comparison shopping means comparing the prices of products to find the best buy.

A **brand** is the name of a product or the name of a company that makes a product.

57

VOCABULARY: Matching

Match the word or phrase in Group B with a definition in Group A.
Write the letter of the answer on the line.

Group A	Group B
_____ **1.** These tell you to buy products. You find them on TV and in newspapers.	**a.** classified ads
	b. advertisements
_____ **2.** This label means that the product is made by a well-known company.	**c.** name brand
_____ **3.** To find a used appliance, you would read this section of the newspaper.	**d.** unit price
	e. store brand
_____ **4.** A product that is sold only at one kind of store will be labeled with this.	
_____ **5.** The price of one ounce or one pound of a product is called this.	

COMPREHENSION: Finish the Paragraph

Use the following words or phrases to finish the paragraph.
Write the words you choose on the correct lines.

washed
labels
coupons
comparison
brands
shopper
dry clean

You can save money by being a smart _____ .

Compare the prices of different _____ to see

which is the best buy. When you compare prices, you are

_____ shopping. You can also use _____

to pay less for food. Read clothing _____ to find

out if you should wash or _____ the clothes. You

save money by buying clothes that can be _____ .

 **THINKING AND WRITING** Think about how you shop. How do you decide what to buy? How do you pick one product over another? How can you become a better shopper? Explain your answers in your journal.

BUYING INSURANCE

Think About As You Read

- How can health insurance protect you?
- Why do you need insurance for your home and car?
- How can you buy insurance wisely?

Pam just started a new job. She took this job because she could earn more money. Pam also liked her new company's health **insurance** plan. If she gets sick, her insurance will help pay for her doctors and medicine. It will pay for most of her stay in a hospital. Without insurance, Pam could not afford to pay for health care.

There are many different kinds of insurance. You can get insurance for your health, home, life, and car. Insurance keeps you from losing too much money when you have special problems or

Insurance helps pay the cost of accidents and sicknesses.

Find out if you can get health insurance where you work.

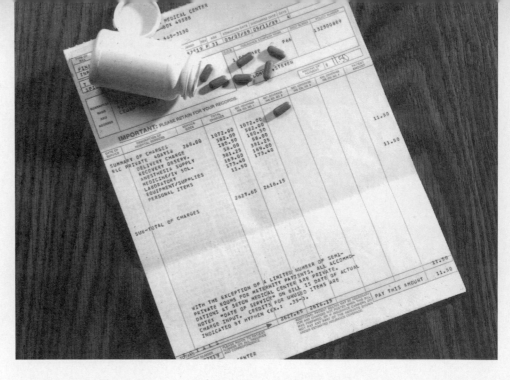

Health insurance can help pay hospital bills.

Surgery is the use of medical tools to operate on the body.

Benefits are the money your insurance company pays you.

accidents. It is important to understand how insurance works and how to buy it if you need it.

Health Insurance

Health care is very expensive. Health insurance helps you pay for good health care. There are different kinds of health insurance. **Hospitalization** pays most of the cost of staying in a hospital. **Medical insurance** helps you pay your doctor bills. It also pays for medicines and different kinds of tests. You need both types of health insurance.

Major medical is the third type of health insurance. It pays very large medical bills. This insurance will pay for expensive tests and **surgery**. A very sick person may have medical bills that cost thousands of dollars. Few people can afford to pay these large bills. You need major medical insurance in case you need to pay large medical bills.

Health insurance can be expensive. So most people try to join group health insurance plans. Group plans cost less. They often pay better **benefits**. Many companies offer group health insurance plans to their workers. Government jobs also offer group health insurance. Find out if you can get group health insurance where you work.

Home Insurance

Imagine what would happen if a fire destroyed the inside of your home. Almost everything you own would be destroyed. Would you have enough money to buy all the things that you lost? That is why you need insurance for your home. If you own a house, you need homeowner's insurance. If you rent an apartment, you need renter's insurance.

The insurance **policy** you buy for your home protects you in other ways. It protects you if your home is robbed. It pays the medical bills if visitors get hurt in your home. It pays the cost if you damage someone else's property. Insurance for your home covers many problems.

Life Insurance

You may want to buy life insurance to protect your family. Your life insurance policy will pay benefits to your family after you die. These benefits will help your family pay for what they need.

Who needs life insurance? Most married people need insurance. People who have children need life insurance.

Many people may not need life insurance. Most people who do not have children may not need it. Many single people may not need it.

A **policy** is an agreement or contract with an insurance company. The policy tells how much you must pay for protection. It also tells the benefits you may receive.

Home insurance can help pay for damage caused by fire.

There are two kinds of life insurance. They are **term insurance** and **whole life insurance**. Term insurance pays benefits only if you die. The cost of term insurance gets higher as people grow older. After age seventy, people cannot have term insurance. Whole life is life insurance with a savings plan. It often costs much more than term insurance. You can have a whole life policy for as long as you live. You can use the savings money as an older adult. This type of plan also pays benefits to your family when you die.

Many people with young families buy term insurance. They get more protection for their families for less money.

Car Insurance

In many states you must buy car insurance if you have a car. Maybe you live in a state without this law. Even if you do, you need car insurance to protect yourself.

It is important to have car insurance.

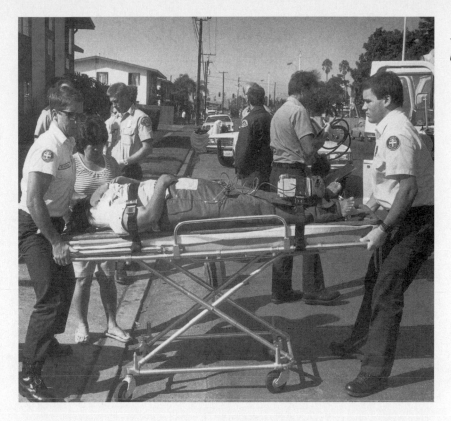

Insurance can help if you are in an accident.

Your car insurance policy should give you several kinds of protection. **Liability insurance** is the most important kind. Liability protects you if your car damages another car or person. It protects you if your car crashes into the property of another person. Your insurance company will pay for the damages. Buy as much liability insurance as you can afford.

Your car insurance policy will help you if you are in a car accident. It can pay to repair the damage to your car. It can pay small medical bills for people who were hurt in the accident. You may also get benefits if you are unable to work because of the accident.

Buying Insurance

Your goal when buying insurance is to get as much protection as you can and not spend too much money. Buy only as much insurance as you need.

You can buy insurance from an insurance **agent**. Some agents work for only one company.

An **agent** is a person who sells insurance from one or more companies.

69

Others sell insurance for a few different companies. Sometimes you can find an agent from a friend or family member. The agent should understand your needs. The agent should help you understand different kinds of policies. After you buy a policy, your agent should explain all of its benefits to you.

Always buy insurance from a good company. There are books in the library that tell you about different insurance companies. These books grade the companies. The best insurance companies get a grade of A or A+. Buy your policy from one of these companies.

Comparison shopping can help you save money on insurance. Check to see which company will give you the best protection. You also want the best price.

Plan your budget so that you have money to pay for the insurance you need. Think about your insurance needs. Then try to get the best policy you can find for your money.

Discuss your insurance needs with an agent.

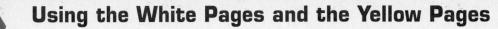

Using the White Pages and the Yellow Pages

The White Pages

The white pages of a phone book list people and businesses and their phone numbers. People are listed by their last names. Next to each name is an address and telephone number. Names are listed in **alphabetical order**. They are listed in the order of letters of the alphabet.

How do you find the name you need in the white pages? At the top of each page are two guide names. The name on the left is the first name on the page. The name on the right is the last name on the page. Use the guide names to find the page you need. Then look for the name you need on that page. Sometimes several people have the same last names. These last names will be listed in the alphabetical order of their first names. On page 298, Jack Karlin comes before Steven Karlin.

Karas - Kaufman	**298**
Karas Rugs & Carpets	Karpinsky Richard B 33 Windsor St 426-8331
276 Main St **489-2000**	Karre Erwin 155 Grand Av 295-3800
Karasz B 35 N Village Av 681-3078	Karron Bernard 60 Rose St 968-5711
Karavitch W & H 15 Murfield Rd....................243-3141	Karst O 7 Shepherd Dr.................................986-4922
Kardon Ron 3 Mills Av....................................539-0456	Kashinsky Ian DDS 43 Ocean St 324-7299
Kardonsky S M 44 Wanamaker Rd 889-5231	Kasman G 199 Kings Ct................................244-7700
Kareckas R J 6 Rome Av................................203-5156	Kasoff Daniel 116 Blenco Ct 864-3729
Karen Ansell Atty 19 Nevins St 621-1720	Kasper J 451 Reina St..................................243-4488
Karger Allan 235 Arizona Pl...........................763-3003	Kass Edward 131 Vernon Av 432-3086
Karhan Joseph 12 Barbara La 941-5117	Kasof Ed 33 Dalton Ct..................................889-1993
Karhu John 11 Park St....................................887-4236	Kassover James 402 Inwood Av 897-0100
Karl William G 49 Derrick Av 889-2491	Kasten Avi 335 Spruce St 241-6783
Karlin Jack 33 Tulip St....................................982-3706	Kasten Carmi 302 Maple St 432-9100
Karlin Steven 93 Shore Av 465-4110	Kathman Richard 2926 Davis Av 876-2000
Karmel R 8 Forestdale Rd..............................971-0507	Katkin Marvin 28 Willard Av..........................992-3845
Karmen L 301 Ocean St.................................866-5692	Kaufman David 190 Oceanside Rd...............936-0991
Karmen Morton 50 New St..............................966-1193	Kaufman Estelle 96 Elm Dr...........................966-8023
Karolee Insurance Agency	Kaufman Frank 92 Mildred St.........................436-6651
10 London Pl....................................**491-0451**	Kaufman George MD 2 Lines Rd...................966-4040

Find the telephone numbers for the following people and businesses.

1. Steven Karlin _____

2. Karolee Insurance _____

3. David Kaufman _____

4. George Kaufman _____

The Yellow Pages

You can use the yellow pages to find a business, store, or service. Businesses are listed under headings in the yellow pages. Perhaps you want to find an insurance agent. You would look under the heading *Insurance*. Headings are listed in alphabetical order. Businesses are listed in alphabetical order under each heading. Some businesses also have ads under the heading.

Insurance 314

● **INSURANCE (Cont'd)**

CNA Insurance
AGENT
GROBER IMBEY AGENCY INC
See Ad Page 311
1907 Green St..................................622-8300

CARBONE/ORRINO AGENCY INC
See Ad Page 308
15 Village Av...................................896-1800

CESIRO ASSOCIATES INC
See Ad Page 312
175 Grand St...................................498-4000

Clark Joseph D
500 Henry St...................................763-1555

D'Amato Joseph
265 Sun St......................................868-4100

Devincenzo & Dickerson Inc
45 Nevins Av...................................223-8000

Diplomat Agency Inc
75 Main St......................................379-5260

Durnan Brindley Agency Inc The
3311 Clinton Av...............................869-9999

Evans International Inc
1371 Ford Pl...................................326-9222

Executive Fringe Concepts Inc
7100 Walden Dr...............................486-9000

F M Associates Limited
1100 Hall Rd...................................535-1001

Firestone Agency Inc
5926 Burton Av................................268-2000

● **INSURANCE (Cont'd)**

Health Masters Inc
119 N Park Av..................................926-1000

Home Insurance Companies
AGENT
CESIRO ASSOCIATES INC
See Ad Page 313
11 Atlantic St..................................889-1426

Horizon Insurance Agency Ltd
37 White Rd.....................................432-8900

Independent Insurance Agents
MEMBER
RUCHMAN ASSOC
121 Morris Av..................................383-5300

Infofacts Inc
30 Lincoln Dr...................................644-1111

Innovative Monetary Designs Ltd
56 Laro St.......................................738-2000

Jaffee Nat Insurance Agency
9703 Motor St..................................738-2190

Karolee Insurance Agency
10 London Pl...................................491-0451

Katsh Brokerage Inc
400 Sun Pl......................................988-1000

Kempen
BUSINESS INSURANCE AGENT
KRASNER LOUIS D INC
Workers Compensation Insurance
379 Westhaven Dr............................647-7000

Find the telephone numbers of the following businesses.

1. Firestone Agency _____

2. Health Masters _____

3. Joseph D. Clark _____

4. CNA Insurance _____

▶ WORKSHOP PRACTICE: Use the White and Yellow Pages

Look back at the white pages and yellow pages in the Life Skills Workshop. Use those pages to answer these questions.

1. How many people have the same last name of Kasten? (white pages)

   _____

2. What is Bernard Karron's telephone number? (white pages) _____

3. What are two businesses on page 298 of the white pages?

   _____

   _____

4. What is the telephone number and address of the Diplomat Agency?

   (yellow pages) _____

5. What is the telephone number and address of the Horizon Insurance

   Agency? (yellow pages) _____

   _____

6. On what page would you find an ad for the Carbone/Orrino Agency?

   (yellow pages) _____

▶ COMPREHENSION: Write the Answer

Write one or more sentences to answer each question.

1. What is the best way to buy health insurance?

   _____

   _____

2. Why do you need insurance for your home?

   _____

   _____

3. Who needs life insurance? Who does not need it?

_____

_____

4. How does car insurance protect you?

_____

_____

VOCABULARY: Finish the Sentence

Choose one of the following words or phrases to complete each sentence. Write the word or phrase on the correct line.

benefit
liability insurance
agent
policy
major medical

1. Very large medical bills can be paid by _____ insurance.

2. The money you are paid by your insurance company is called a _____ .

3. A person who sells insurance from one or more companies is an _____ .

4. Your contract with an insurance company that states your payments and benefits is called a

   _____ .

5. If you have caused damage to another person or to the person's property, the damages can be paid with

   _____ .

THINKING AND WRITING Which types of insurance do you think you need? How will you buy policies to meet your needs? Explain your answers in your journal.

OWNING A CAR

Think About As You Read

▶ How do you shop for a new car?

▶ What do you look for when buying a used car?

▶ What do you look for when shopping for a car loan?

Jessica needs to buy a car. She does not know if she should buy a new car or a used one. She knows she will need a loan to pay for her car. Jessica does not know how to find a loan with low interest rates. You may face these same problems if you decide to buy a car.

Buying a New Car

New cars often have fewer problems than used cars. As cars get older, their parts begin to wear out. They may need expensive repairs. Most new cars do not have these problems during the first few years.

Check the sticker prices on new cars.

Talk to the salesperson to negotiate the price of the car you want.

Options are extra items you can buy for a new car.

Dealers are businesses that sell certain brands of cars.

Negotiate means to talk over and agree on something together.

If you get a new car, you can order the kind of car you want. You can choose the car's color. You can buy **options** to make the car have the features you want.

A visit to your library can help you decide what kind of new car to buy. You will find books and magazines that tell you about different car models. They tell you which cars may need few repairs. They also tell you about the prices of different car models. You can use the information you get at the library to help you shop for a car.

How can you get the best price when you buy a new car? Visit a few car **dealers**. Find out the price of the same car at different dealers. Then you can **negotiate** the price with a salesperson. You do not have to agree to the first price that the salesperson offers. Often, a salesperson will lower the price to make sure you do not go to another dealer for a better price.

Every new car comes with a **warranty**. The warranty is a promise to repair most of the car's problems for a certain period of time. Sometimes a warranty protects the car for a certain number of miles. Some warranties are for as long as seven years or 70,000 miles. This means that most repairs will be done without charge for the first seven years or for 70,000 miles. A good warranty can save the buyer a lot of money.

Check your new car carefully before driving it home. Make sure all the controls work correctly. Have the dealer fix all problems before you drive home. Have the salesperson explain the warranty to you.

Buying a Used Car

Every year more used cars are sold than new cars. Used cars cost much less than new cars. Car insurance is also cheaper for a used car. You can buy a used car from new and used car dealers. You can also buy one from a person who wants to sell his or her old car.

Try to get a used car that has been well cared for. You can get information about different models of used cars in the library. Books and magazines can tell you which used car models are most likely to have problems. Avoid buying those models.

You can buy a used car from the owner.

A **mechanic** is a worker who uses tools to repair cars and other machines.

A used car may have many more problems than a new car. It may look beautiful and shiny. But the used car may not work properly. It may need many expensive repairs.

Check the used car carefully for problems. It is best to check the car during the day. The car should have good paint and no rust marks. It should have five good tires. Try to find out if the car was in an accident. Avoid buying cars that have been in accidents. Always test drive the car.

You may find a used car that you really like. Have a **mechanic** check it for problems. You can buy the car if you get a good report. Do not buy the car if your mechanic says it needs expensive repairs.

Always negotiate the price of a used car. Some people save hundreds of dollars by bargaining for a fair price.

Have a mechanic you trust check out the used car before you buy it.

Paying for Your Car

You can buy a car with money you have saved. Or you can get a car loan to buy a car. Before shopping for a car, know how much you can afford to spend. Your budget may include a certain amount for monthly car payments. Decide how much money you have for a down payment. Then shop for a loan for the amount you plan to spend.

Shop carefully for your car loan. Check the interest rates at banks, credit unions, and car dealers. You want to get the lowest interest rate you can find. The length of time you need to pay back a loan also affects the interest rate. You will pay much more interest on longer loans. You will also have to pay a higher interest rate on a loan for a used car.

The interest you pay for your car loan will make your car cost more. Jessica needed a $5,000 loan to buy her car. She took out a three-year, or 36-month, loan. She paid 9 percent interest. Over three years,

When you **register** a car, you list it in the records of the state motor vehicle department.

A **motor vehicle department** in a state controls the state's laws for driver's licenses, registering cars, and traffic safety.

A **collision** is a crash. Collision insurance pays for the repairs a car needs after a crash.

Jessica will have to pay about $5,723 because of the interest charges. Suppose Jessica had taken a loan that charged 18 percent interest? After three years, she would have paid about $6,500 because of the interest. Always comparison shop for a loan.

Owning Your Car

Register your car with your state's **motor vehicle department**. In some states, you must buy car insurance in order to register your car. Check with the motor vehicle department in your state to learn how to register your car. Some states also have laws that cars must pass a state inspection each year.

You will want to have the right kind of car insurance for your car. In Chapter 7 you read about different kinds of car insurance. If you buy a new or nearly new car, you need **collision** insurance. This type of insurance will pay to repair your car if you

MONTHLY LOAN PAYMENTS							
		2-year Loan			3-year Loan		
Amount of Loan	Interest Rate	Interest to be Paid	Monthly Payment	Total to Repay	Interest to be Paid	Monthly Payment	Total to Repay
$1,000	10%	$200	$50	$1,200	$300	$36	$1,300
	12%	$240	$51	$1,240	$360	$37	$1,360
	18%	$360	$56	$1,360	$540	$42	$1,540
$2,500	10%	$500	$125	$3,000	$750	$90	$3,250
	12%	$600	$129	$3,100	$900	$94	$3,400
	18%	$900	$141	$3,400	$1,350	$106	$3,850

Note: Interest and monthly payments were calculated using simple interest. Actual payments and interest would be less on installment loans.

Your monthly loan payment depends on three things: the amount of the loan, the interest rate, and the length of the loan.

are in an accident. If you buy an older car, you may not need this insurance. Most insurance companies will not pay to repair older cars. Ask your insurance agent about the kind of insurance that you need.

Every car needs care. It is important to change your car's oil every few thousand miles. Change the oil at least twice a year. Your tires also need the correct amount of air. So check the air in your tires. Always check that your brakes work well. If you do not know how to care for a car yourself, take it to a good mechanic. Or you can take a basic car care course to learn.

Buying and owning a car takes time and money. You need to decide whether to buy a new car or a used car. You may need to get a loan to pay for your car. You may need to register and insure it. Then you will have to take care of your car to keep it running well.

Take good care of your car to make it last.

LIFE SKILLS Workshop

Completing a Car Loan Application

Look at the sample car loan application on page 83. It was filled out by Jessica. Notice the following parts.

 Type of Credit. Sometimes two people apply for a loan together. They apply for "joint credit." Each person has to fill out a separate form. If one person cannot repay the loan, then the other person has to repay it.

 Personal Information. Your **dependents** are the people you must take care of. This part asks for the name of a family member not living with you. If you move and do not pay your loan, the loan company will try to find you through this family member.

 Employment and Income. Your **gross annual salary** is how much your job pays you each year before taxes are taken out.

 Credit Information. This part asks if you have had any problems repaying loans or if you have gone to court because of money problems. The **title** is the paper that proves who owns the car. The name on the title is the owner of the car.

 Authorization and Disclosure. When you sign this form, it means you will let the credit company check your credit.

▼▼▼

Use Jessica's application to answer the following questions.

1. Will Jessica be the only person responsible for the loan? _____

2. How many dependents does Jessica have? _____

3. How much rent does Jessica pay each month? _____

4. How long has Jessica worked at her job? _____

5. How does Jessica earn extra money? _____

6. Has Jessica ever filed for bankruptcy? _____

7. Has Jessica ever filed for credit under another name? _____

Dollarbank Car Loan Application

1. ☑ I am applying for credit in my own name and I am *not* relying on the income or assets of another person for the repayment of the credit requested.
   ☐ I am applying for credit in my own name and I *am* relying on the income from alimony, child support or separate maintenance *or* the income or assets of another person for the repayment of the credit requested.
   ☐ I am applying for *joint credit* with another person. **NOTE:** A separate credit application must be completed for each applicant.

2. PERSONAL INFORMATION

First Name	Middle Initial	Last Name	Date of Birth	Social Security Number	Number of Dependents
Jessica	J.	Smith	1-29-56	114-76-5276	2

Street Address	City	State	Zip	Phone	
21 Delta Avenue	Miami	FL	33156	(305)297-5401	☐ Own ☐ Parents ☑ Rent ☐ Other

Time at Address	Monthly Mtg./Rent Payment	Landlord or Mortgage Holder
Yrs. 1 Mo. 3	$ 295	John Costello

Previous address if less than 3 years at current address
142 Nelson Street   Miami, FL   33156   How long Yrs. 3 Mo. 3

Name and address of nearest relative not living with you
Mary Cooper   11 Second St.   Atlanta, GA   30344   Phone (404)674-5953

3. EMPLOYMENT AND INCOME

Self Emp. ☐Yes ☑No   Name and address of current employer
Retired ☐Yes ☑No   East Winds Nursing Home 43 Jackson St. Miami   How long Yrs. 1 Mo. 7

Type of Business	Position/Title	Gross Annual Salary	Phone
Nursing Home	Nurse's Aide	$ 18,300	(305)469-2000

Previous employer if less than 3 years on current job
Maple Gardens Nursing Home   How long Yrs. 2 Mo. 4

Other Income Note: Alimony, child support or separate maintenance incomes need not be revealed unless you wish to have such sources considered as a basis for repayment of requested credit.

Other Annual Monthly $ 300   Describe Income Source   Part-time waitress

4. CREDIT INFORMATION

Name and Address of Credit References	Acct. Number	Balance	Monthly Payment
Checking Dollarbank 12 Carson Ave. Miami	030030761	$1,500	
Savings Dollarbank 12 Carson Ave. Miami	010582493	$2,690	
Auto/Installment Loan Information			

Business Checking		Branch	Contact

Credit Cards ☐ American Express ☑ Visa   Other Lang's Dept. Store   Other
☐ Diners Club ☐ Carte Blanche ☑ MasterCard   Other   Other

Are you obligated to make alimony, child support or separate maintenance payments? ☑No ☐ Yes If yes, mo. pmt. $

Have you ever had any vehicle repossessed or any judgments, foreclosures or garnishments filed against you? ☑No ☐ Yes If yes, when?

Have you ever filed for bankruptcy? ☑No ☐ Yes If yes, when?

Have you ever applied for credit in another name? ☐ No ☑Yes If yes, what name? Jessica Clark

Vehicle to be titled in the name of: Jessica Smith   Relationship self

5. AUTHORIZATION AND DISCLOSURE

Applicant's Statement

Every statement I have made in this application is true and correct and has been made by me with the understanding that you will rely on it. I agree that if anything arises which changes any of the statements I have made, I will promptly tell you. You may exchange credit information about me with others. Dollarbank normally obtains credit reports for all loan applications, and for updates, renewals or extensions of credit granted. Upon request, Dollarbank will inform me if a report has been obtained and will give me the name and address of the agency furnishing the report.

Jessica Smith   4-29-94
Applicant's Signature   Date

▶ WORKSHOP PRACTICE: Complete a Car Loan Application

Practice your skills at filling out forms. Fill out this car loan form for yourself. Look back at pages 82 and 83 to help you complete this form.

<table>
<tr><td rowspan="7">P E R S O N A L
I N F O R M A T I O N</td><td>First Name</td><td>Middle Initial</td><td colspan="2">Last Name</td><td>Date of Birth</td><td colspan="2">Social Security Number</td><td>Number of Dependents</td></tr>
<tr><td colspan="2">Street Address</td><td>City</td><td>State   Zip</td><td colspan="2">Phone
(   )</td><td>☐ Own ☐ Parents
☐ Rent ☐ Other</td></tr>
<tr><td colspan="2">Time at Address
Yrs. _____ Mo. _____</td><td>Monthly Mtg./Rent Payment
$</td><td colspan="4">Landlord or Mortgage Holder</td></tr>
<tr><td colspan="6">Previous address if less than 3 years at current address</td><td colspan="2">How long
Yrs. ____ Mo. ____</td></tr>
<tr><td colspan="6">Name and address of nearest relative not living with you</td><td colspan="2">Phone
(   )</td></tr>
</table>

<table>
<tr><td rowspan="6">E M P L O Y M E N T
A N D
I N C O M E</td><td>Self Emp. ☐Yes ☐No</td><td colspan="5">Name and address of current employer</td><td>How long
Yrs. ____ Mo. ____</td></tr>
<tr><td>Retired   ☐Yes ☐No</td></tr>
<tr><td colspan="2">Type of Business</td><td colspan="2">Position/Title</td><td>Gross Annual Salary
$</td><td colspan="2">Phone
(   )</td></tr>
<tr><td colspan="6">Previous employer if less than 3 years on current job</td><td colspan="2">How long
Yrs. ____ Mo. ____</td></tr>
<tr><td colspan="8">**Other Income Note:** Alimony, child support or separate maintenance incomes need not be revealed unless you wish to have such sources considered as a basis for repayment of requested credit.</td></tr>
<tr><td colspan="2">Other Annual
Monthly $</td><td colspan="6">Describe
Income Source</td></tr>
</table>

<table>
<tr><td rowspan="12">C R E D I T
I N F O R M A T I O N</td><td colspan="2">Name and Address of Credit References</td><td>Acct. Number</td><td>Balance</td><td>Monthly Payment</td></tr>
<tr><td colspan="2">Checking</td><td></td><td></td><td></td></tr>
<tr><td colspan="2">Savings</td><td></td><td></td><td></td></tr>
<tr><td colspan="2">Auto/Installment Loan Information</td><td></td><td></td><td></td></tr>
<tr><td colspan="2"></td><td></td><td></td><td></td></tr>
<tr><td colspan="2">Business Checking</td><td></td><td>Branch</td><td>Contact</td></tr>
<tr><td colspan="2">Credit Cards   ☐ American Express   ☐ Visa   Other</td><td colspan="3">Other</td></tr>
<tr><td colspan="2">☐ Diners Club ☐ Carte Blanche   ☐ MasterCard   Other</td><td colspan="3">Other</td></tr>
<tr><td colspan="2">Are you obligated to make alimony, child support or separate maintenance payments?
☐ No   ☐ Yes   If yes, mo. pmt. $</td><td colspan="3">Have you ever had any vehicle repossessed or any judgments, foreclosures or garnishments filed against you? ☐ No ☐ Yes
If yes, when?</td></tr>
<tr><td colspan="2">Have you ever filed for bankruptcy?
☐No   ☐ Yes   If yes, when?</td><td colspan="3">Have you ever applied for credit in another name?   ☐ No   ☐ Yes
If yes, what name?</td></tr>
<tr><td colspan="5">Vehicle to be titled
in the name of:

                                                                    Relationship</td></tr>
</table>

▶ VOCABULARY: Writing with Vocabulary Words

Use five or more of the following words to write a paragraph that tells how to buy a used car carefully.

dealers
insurance
negotiate
mechanic
collision
warranty
register

_____

_____

_____

_____

_____

_____

▶ COMPREHENSION: Circle the Answer

Draw a circle around the correct answer.

1. A new car comes with a _____ that says repairs will be made without charge for a certain period of time.

insurance   warranty   loan

2. Interest rates on a loan for a new car are often _____ than on a used car.

higher   lower

3. You will pay less interest on a car loan that you take for _____ months.

24   36   48

4. People may not need collision insurance for very _____ cars.

old   new   large

5. A used car should be checked for problems by a _____ before you buy it.

bank   insurance agent   mechanic

 THINKING AND WRITING Sometimes it is hard to decide whether to buy a new car or a used one. Which kind of car would you buy and why? Where would you go to get information about the car you are thinking of buying? What would you do to get a good car at a fair price? Explain your answer in your journal.

CROSSWORD PUZZLE: Wheeling and Dealing

Use the clues to complete the crossword puzzle.

Choose from the following words.

For an extra challenge, cover up the words.

agent
comparison
generic
hospitalization
negotiate
options
policy
warranty

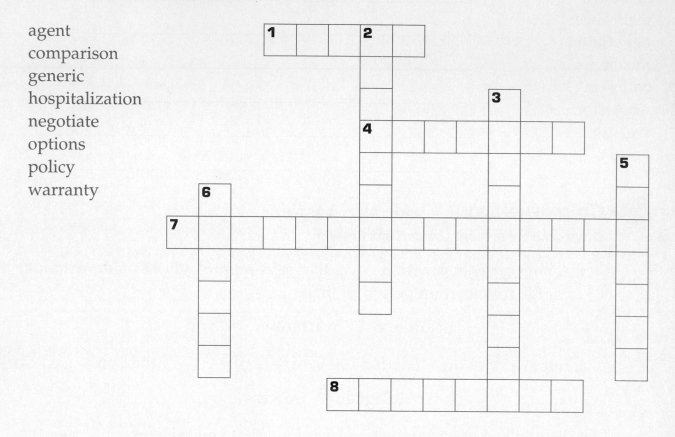

Across

1. An _ _ _ _ _ is a person who sells insurance.

4. _ _ _ _ _ are extra items you can buy for a new car.

7. _ _ _ _ _ is insurance that pays a large part of the cost of staying in the hospital.

8. A _ _ _ _ _ for a car is a promise to make certain repairs without charge for a certain period of time.

Down

2. To _ _ _ _ _ means to talk over and agree on something together.

3. _ _ _ _ _ shopping means comparing the prices of products to find the best buy.

5. Products that are _ _ _ _ _ have no company name and come in a plain wrapper.

6. A _ _ _ _ _ is an agreement or contract with an insurance company.

Glossary

A

advertisements Ads that tell you what is special about a product. page 57

agent A person who sells insurance. page 69

alphabetical order Using the first letters of words to put them in the order of the letters of the alphabet. page 71

annual salary The amount of money you earn from your job each year. page 32

appliances Machines that make work easier, such as stoves. page 60

application A written form you fill out to apply for something, such as a credit card. page 28

automated teller machine (ATM) A machine that allows you to get money from your bank account at any time. page 9

B

balance The amount of money you have in your account. page 17

benefits The money your insurance company pays you. page 66

billing period The total number of days a bill covers. Charges made before or after the billing period appear on a different bill. page 47

brand The name of a product or the name of a company that makes a product. page 57

budget A plan for spending money and saving money. page 36

budget checking account A low-cost checking account for people who write only a few checks each month. page 17

C

canceled checks Checks that are marked to show that money was withdrawn to pay for the check. The check cannot be used again. page 16

Certificate of Deposit (CD) A type of savings account that often earns more interest than a regular savings account. Money must be kept in the account for a certain period of time. page 7

checkbook register A book used to record all the checks and deposits of a checking account. page 18

checking account A bank account that allows you to take money out of the bank by writing checks. page 8

classified ads Lists in the newspaper of used products for sale. page 61

closing date The last day that charges can be added to a bill. page 50

collision insurance Insurance that pays for the repairs a car needs after a crash. page 80

comparison shopping Comparing the prices of products to find the best buy. page 57

consumer A person who buys and uses products and services. page 4

credit Borrowing money to buy goods now and pay for them later. page 26

credit cards Cards that let you buy goods and pay for them after you get the bill. page 27

credit rating How well you pay back the money you have borrowed. page 29

customer service representative A worker who helps you use services. page 9

D

dealers Businesses that sell certain brands of new and used cars. page 76

debits Charges that are subtracted from your account balance. page 22

debt Money borrowed from and owed to a person or business. page 29

dependents The people an adult takes care of. page 82

deposit To put money into an account. page 9

down payment The first payment for a product bought with credit. A down payment pays only part of the cost of the product. page 30

due date The day that your bill payment must be received by the company. page 30

E

endorse To write your signature on the back of a check to show that you want cash or credit for the amount of the check. page 11

expenses All the things you pay for. page 37

F

F.D.I.C. The Federal Deposit Insurance Corporation, the government agency that protects the money you have saved in the bank so it will not be lost or stolen. page 6

fee The money charged for a service. page 17

finance charge The interest added to a credit card bill when you do not pay the full balance due. page 47

fixed income Earning the same amount of money each month. page 37

G

generic brands Products with no company name and plain wrappers. page 58

gross annual salary The amount your job pays you each year before taxes are taken out. page 82

H

hardships Hard times and troubles. page 46

hospitalization insurance Insurance that pays a large part of the cost of staying in the hospital. page 66

I

identification A paper or card that proves who you are. page 9

impress To affect the way others think and feel. page 56

influence To change the ideas and actions of others. page 56

installment plan A plan that allows you to buy a product and pay for it in monthly payments with interest. page 30

insufficient funds Not having enough money in your bank account to cover your checks. page 19

insurance A plan to help pay the cost of accidents and sicknesses. page 65

interest The money paid for using someone else's money. You can earn interest on money that you save. You pay interest on money that you borrow. page 5

J

joint checking account A bank account that belongs to two people. page 18

L

liability insurance Insurance that pays for damages you cause to another person or to the person's property. page 69

M

maiden name The family name that a woman used as a child. page 9

major credit cards Credit cards that are prepared by banks and that can be used in many different businesses. page 27

major medical insurance Insurance that pays for very large medical bills such as surgery. page 66

mechanic A worker who uses tools to repair cars and other machines. page 78

medical insurance Insurance that helps pay the cost of doctor bills, medicines, and blood tests. page 66

minimum balance The least amount you can have in your account without being charged a fee. page 17

minimum payment The least amount you can pay on a bill. page 30

motor vehicle department A state agency that controls the state's laws for driver's licenses, registering cars, and traffic safety. page 80

N

name brand A product made by a well-known company and sold in many different stores. page 58

negotiate To talk over and agree on something together. You can negotiate a car's price with a salesperson. page 76

O

options Extra items you can buy for a new car. Air-conditioning is an option on some cars. page 76

overdraft A check written for more money than is in your checking account. page 19

overdrawn When you do not have enough money in your account to cover your checks. page 19

P

payee The person or company to whom a check is written. page 19

policy An agreement or contract with an insurance company. The policy tells how much you must pay for protection. It also tells the benefits you may receive. page 67

position The kind of work you do. page 32

R

register To list a car in the records of the state motor vehicle department. page 80

renter's insurance Insurance that protects you if you rent an apartment. page 38

retirement The period of time when an older person no longer works or when a person leaves a job after many years. page 6

S

safe deposit box A metal box that holds important papers and other items so they cannot be stolen or damaged by fire. It is kept in a bank's vault or safe. page 8

savings account A bank account that earns money for you while keeping the money safe. page 5

social security number A number that shows that you are part of the social security system. This system gives money to older people and to the disabled. page 9

stability Staying in one place for a long time. page 32

stop payment When a bank does not withdraw money from your checking account to pay for the check. Banks often stop payment on stolen checks. page 16

store brand A product sold only in one kind of store. page 58

surgery The use of medical tools to operate on the body. page 66

T

term insurance Life insurance that pays money to your family if you die when the insurance is in effect. page 68

title The paper that proves who owns a car. page 82

transfer To move money from one account into another. page 17

U

unit price The price of one ounce, one pound, or other measurement of a product. page 62

W

warranty A promise to make certain repairs without charge for a certain period of time. page 76

whole life insurance Life insurance that has a savings plan. page 68

withdraw To take money out of a bank account. page 7

withdrawal form A paper you fill out to tell the bank to take money out of your account. page 12

Y

yearly income All the money you receive during a year. page 32

INDEX

Chapter 1

Page 11 Workshop

1. Michael Miller   **4.** 9415393

2. savings   **5.** $35.10

3. 1–12–94   **6.** 2

Page 12 Workshop

1. Ninety-two   **4.** $32.00

2. 2–10–94   **5.** 9415393

3. $60.00   **6.** $92.00

Page 13 Workshop Practice

N National Savings Bank				Withdrawal	
Withdrawal Amount (In Words)	*Eighty – nine*				Dollars
Date *today's date*	Signature *your signature*				
Please Issue Money Order(s) in the amount(s) of:			Dollars	Cents	Below for bank use only. Money Order/Official Check #
			61	25	
		Cash ▶	27	75	No Book ☐
Account Number 3 2 5 6 2 1 9		Total Withdrawal	89	00	Passbook Balance After Update

Pages 13–14 Comprehension

1. People want to keep money in a savings account because their money will earn interest and it will be safe.

2. Services that banks offer include savings accounts, checking accounts, safe deposit boxes, automated teller machines, money orders, and loans. (Any four are correct.)

3. Banks earn money by charging interest on loans.

4. You decide which bank to use by finding a bank that charges higher interest on savings accounts and less money for other services. You may want a bank that is nearby, open on Saturdays, or open late at night.

Page 14 Vocabulary

1. withdrawal form   **4.** retirement

2. interest   **5.** identification

3. maiden name   **6.** deposit

Chapter 2

Page 20 Workshop

1. 1–27–94

2. Marcy's Department Store

3. $21.76, Twenty-one and 76/100

4. a sweater

Page 21 Workshop

1. 1–17   **4.** $205

2. $300   **5.** $150

3. 102

Page 22 Workshop

1. $184.94   **4.** 4

2. $0.00   **5.** 1–31–94

3. 2   **6.** 1–30

7. and 8.

Item No. or Trans. Code	Date	TRANSACTION DESCRIPTION	Subtractions Amount of Payment or Withdrawal (−)		✓ T	(−) Fee if Any	Additions Amount of Deposit or interest (+)	Balance	
	1/17	Built Well Company paycheck			✓		300 00	300 00	balance
101	1/24	Major Telephone monthly bill	26 30		✓			−26 30 273 70	balance
102	1/26	Apartment City rent	205 00		✓			−205 00 68 70	balance
	1/27	M. R. Smith refund			✓		150 00	+150 00 218 70	balance
103	1/27	Marcy's Department Store sweater	21 76		✓			−21 76 196 94	balance
	1/21	Check Order checks	12 00		✓			−12 00 184 94	balance

Yes, the balances match. The balance is $184.94.

Page 24 Workshop Practice

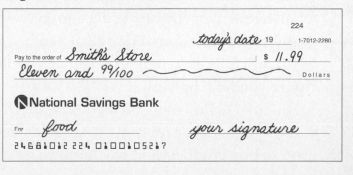

Item No. or Trans. Code	Date	TRANSACTION DESCRIPTION	Subtractions Amount of Payment or Withdrawal (−)		✓ T	(−) Fee if Any	Additions Amount of Deposit or interest (+)	Balance	
								250 00	
223	2/7	Department of Public Safety license renewal	10 00					−10 00 240 00	
224		Smith's Store food	11 99					−11 99 (228 01)	

Page 25 Vocabulary

1. fee
2. balance
3. signature
4. canceled check

Page 25 Comprehension

1. False; It is not safe to mail cash.
2. False; All checking accounts are not the same.
3. True
4. True

Chapter 3

Page 32 Workshop

1. 2 years
2. 06–02–66
3. Greenway Builders
4. construction worker
5. $23,585
6. yes

Page 34 Workshop Practice

The answers on the form will vary. Print clearly and fill out the form completely.

Page 35 Vocabulary

Answers will vary. You may use more than one vocabulary word in a sentence.

Page 35 Comprehension

When you buy a product and pay for it at a later time, you are using <u>credit</u>. You can buy goods in many different stores and be billed for all of them together by using a <u>major credit card</u>. If you cannot pay all of your credit card bills, the credit card company will charge you high <u>interest</u>. If you use your credit cards to buy more than you can afford, you will have <u>debt</u> problems. There are other ways to buy products and pay for them later. You can use an <u>installment plan</u> or get a <u>loan</u> to buy very expensive goods.

Chapter 4

Pages 41–42 Workshop

The budget plan will vary.

Page 43 Workshop Practice

1. $70
2. $5
3. $3
4. $6.50
5. $10

Page 43 Vocabulary

1. d
2. e
3. f
4. c
5. b
6. a

Page 44 Comprehension

1. eating out
2. medical care
3. food
4. renter's insurance
5. car
6. put money in a savings account

Chapter 5

Page 50 Workshop

1. 3/15/94
2. $58.97
3. $20.00
4. $58.97
5. 3
6. $89.00
7. $89.00
8. 21.6%

Page 52 Workshop Practice

1. 5396 9141 0129 2972
2. Feb. 15, 1994
3. $48.86
4. $15.00
5. yes
6. Dollarmaster Card

Pages 52–53 Vocabulary

1. hardships
2. closing date
3. due date
4. finance charge
5. minimum

Page 53 Comprehension

1. False; A finance charge is added to a credit card bill when the full amount is not paid.
2. True
3. True
4. False; When paying credit card bills, it is best to pay the full amount to avoid a finance charge.

Page 54 Crossword Puzzle

```
¹R A T ²I N G                    ³B
      N                          U
    ⁴W I T H D R A W        ⁵D E B T
      E                          G
      R                          E
    ⁶I D E N T I ⁷F I ⁸C A T I O N
      S          I    R
      T          N    E
                 A    D
                 N    I
                 C    T
                 E
```

Chapter 6

Page 62 Workshop

1. 59¢
2. 7.4¢ per ounce
3. $1.92
4. 6.0¢ per ounce
5. 32-ounce container

Page 63 Workshop Practice

1.a. 26¢
1.b. 23¢
1.c. 8-ounce bottle
2.a. 14¢
2.b. 11¢
2.c. 18-ounce jar
3.a. 7¢
3.b. 8¢
3.c. 22-ounce bottle
4.a. 35¢
4.b. 30¢
4.c. 12-ounce bottle

Page 64 Vocabulary

1. b
2. c
3. a
4. e
5. d

Page 64 Comprehension

You can save money by being a smart shopper. Compare the prices of different brands to see which is the best buy. When you compare prices, you are comparison shopping. You can also use coupons to pay less for food. Read clothing labels to find out if you should wash or dry clean the clothes. You save money by buying clothes that can be washed.

Chapter 7

Page 71 Workshop

1. 465–4110
2. 491–0451
3. 936–0991
4. 966–4040

Page 72 Workshop

1. 268–2000
2. 926–1000
3. 763–1555
4. 622–8300

Page 73 Workshop Practice

1. two
2. 968–5711
3. Karas Rugs and Karolee Insurance
4. 379–5260; 75 Main St.
5. 432–8900; 37 White Rd.
6. 308

Pages 73–74 Comprehension

1. The best way to buy health insurance is from an agent who works for a good company. Comparison shop to find the best protection for the best price.

2. You need insurance for your home because you would not be able to replace the things that would be lost in a fire or robbery.

3. Married people and people with children need life insurance. Single people and people without children do not need life insurance.

4. Car insurance protects you if your car damages another car or person. It pays to repair damage to your car. It pays medical bills and benefits in case you cannot work because of a car accident.

Page 74 Vocabulary

1. major medical
2. benefit
3. agent
4. policy
5. liability insurance

Chapter 8

Page 82 Workshop

1. yes
2. 2
3. $295
4. 1 year, 7 months
5. part-time waitress
6. no
7. yes

Page 84 Workshop Practice

The answers on the form will vary. Print clearly and fill out the form completely.

Page 85 Vocabulary

Answers will vary. You may use more than one word in a sentence.

Page 85 Comprehension

1. warranty
2. lower
3. 24
4. old
5. mechanic

Page 86 Crossword Puzzle

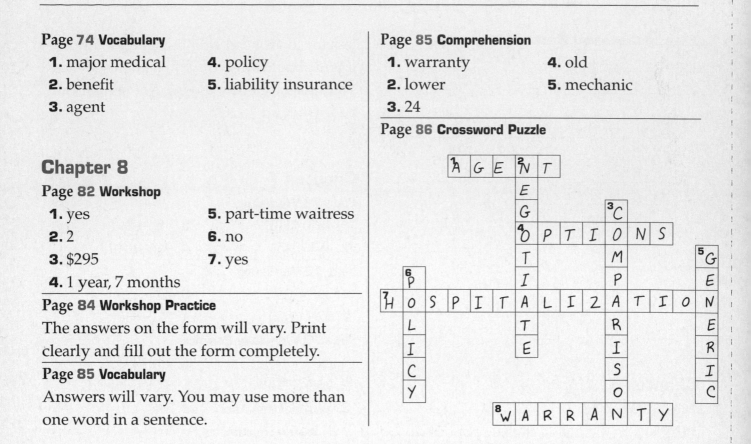